ACKNOWLEDGMENTS

To my fam

I am the child my grandmother a
father aband

To my Aunt Grace, and my Un
forever.

To my friends,

DeAundra, Danielle, Craig, Simon, Sarah.

You kept me going.

To my good friend Randy,

Thank you for producing my lovely promotional photos!

Check out ARRC.
info@arrcmedia.com

To Cindy,

As far apart as we may be in both distance and emotions, our love will forever be immortalized by our words.

From Tim.

To the Universe, with Love

Alex Clennon

TO THE UNIVERSE, WITH LOVE

ISBN: 1541295714
ISBN-13: 978-1541295711

DEDICATION

This one is dedicated to me, for finally having the courage to find true self love and for following my dreams.

CONTENTS

22/12/11

To the Universe,

The heart is the evil dictator who is responsible for the day to day operation of the circulatory system. It stands behind the sternum and barks orders to the arteries and veins in an effort to delegate who is responsible for escorting blood to its sibling organs. Since the proper functionality of the circulatory system is vital to the optimum function of the human body, only a dictator with proper management skills could be best suited for this job. How Heart works, is that he continuously produces a rhythmic beat which sends out the blood which he produces to each organ in the body via the blood vessels. Heart has to take care of its sibling organs like the lungs by using arteries and veins as media to transport food in the form of blood. The heart, along with the brain are the directors of The Human Body; the most powerful and complex information system ever created. Together they under take the tremendous challenge of ensuring that The Human Body is consistently performing at its optimum level of functionality. Now in every Human Body, there is a 'heart' so to speak, which has the same responsibilities as our friend Heart, but each one is different.

In my model of The Human Body, the evil dictator is known as Alex's Heart, who will from now on be referred to as Heart. Now this heart, just like the heart we spoke about previously has the same major responsibility.

For 19 years the heart of my model of the human body has been ensuring that I have been performing without difficulty. Heart carried out his task without error, he ensured that each vessel had work to do each day, and that the work was evenly distributed. No organ went without food at any time during his 19 years of leadership. It's safe to say my heart ran a tight ship.

On October 29, 2011 Heart found a deeper meaning for his life. The brain translated a vision of the most inconceivably beautiful girl the eyes had ever seen. He began to feel feelings he had never felt before. The sight of this mistress lead Heart to increase its beating at first. Heart was confused as he always beat at his own pace, on his own time. But upon the sight of this mistress he couldn't control himself. Heart's irregular beating started to affect the other organs of The Human Body which then started to affect the exterior portion of it. The hands started shaking and emitting a liquid in the palms and the brow of its face. The legs started to fail and the mouth became defective and started to stutter. As the angel started to speak and introduce herself, the fast paced beating went in the opposite direction. The heart started to produce little or no blood. A panic arose in the central tower of the brain and in the central cavity of the chest. The chest began to tighten and experience the most nervous and bittersweet twitch it had ever felt. It was as if someone tickled the lungs. The brain and heart began to feel feelings they had never felt before.

It was as if the brain had lost its footing and the body began to feel as if it were having a sense of euphoria at just the sight and sound of the girl.

The heart then started skipping beats, which lead to the malnourishment of the other organs. The stomach dropped, the liver shook and the bones felt weak. The human body was rendered useless at the sight, sound and thought of this person. Her eyes stared through the eyes of this human body and looked into its soul revealing a side of it that it didn't even know existed. The body felt complete; at peace with itself. It felt as if it had found what it was looking for all its life. The body had found the missing piece to his puzzle.

The heart got his act back together but he still experiences these disruptions from time to time due to the actions of this lady.

This lady changed the life of this body. Her gentle touch erupts a frenzy of irregular beating in the heart, her beautiful ardent eyes sets off a temporary onset of selective amnesia in the brain where it is only able to think tranquil and fulfilling thoughts, her warm tongue causes an explosion of passion from the core of the body which resonates in even its fingertips, and her wise and caring words causes a sense of stability and vision and reason for the body to go on.

With love,

23/10/13

To the Universe,

Love.

To be loved.

To love.

The meaning of life lies above.

So far, I have had five encounters with love. None of which I have come to regret. True love however, I am yet to find. I eagerly await its graceful presence to kiss me upon my cheek with a touch so tender that my heart will surrender.

To date, my third encounter is simply put, puzzling. For some reason, my heart just decided to move on, with scant disregard for what my brain actually wanted.

They don't seem to work together very well.

I thought she was the one.

I thought she was made for me.

Look at what she did to Heart!

Her personality is unmatched. Her beauty is beyond explanation and all comprehension. I met this wonderful woman during my second encounter with love, and I had believed that I fell in love with her at first sight.

My first encounter with love was migrating, and I took my second encounter with love with me to wish her farewell at TGIF. Somewhere during our conversing and well wishing, the girl who was about to dismantle my entire world graced us with her presence. Upon the revelation of her face, my entire body shook and entered a new realm. My eyes were focused solely on her and my mind was focused on the possibility of hearing her voice.

As the Universe would have it, she asked me for a lighter, and my night was made.

I made it my point of duty to be introduced to her, and so said, so done. Our relationship was born out of immorality, and ended as such. I pursued her for four years before our inevitable temporary union. For four years my mind was rattled by our intimate interactions and our heartless separations.

One October, she had invited me to spend the weekend with her in Ocho Rios. It was a popular weekend for Kingstonians to go down. I accepted her request, but upon making plans of my own, I declined on short notice. Quite frankly, I was fed up of her bipolar acceptance and rejection of my love.

We spoke naught for months, leading to years. As fate would have it, a few years later our union was apparently written in the stars. We met up one night, at the place where our path was created. TGIF.

We spoke and she divulged that the weekend that we were supposed to go to Ocho Rios, she was planning to reveal her true feelings to me in the hopes that we would finally foster a true relationship.

As the Universe would have it, the day we met up, was coincident with the day we would have gone to the country in the year we would have gone. As the stars aligned, we had sex that night, and there was born the beginning of a beautiful temporary encounter with true love. This is the closest I have been, and though I am shameful about its end, I couldn't be more appreciative of the moments I shared with this wonderful being.

October 29, 2011 was the day our union became exclusive. I had entered a bartending competition I had won for Jamaica and consequently advanced to the regionals. As fate would have it again, the regionals was in Ocho Rios. We spent that night in the hotel room we would have stayed in had I gone to Ocho Rios with her in the year we were supposed to.

As the competition emerged, my focus was on what was about to unfold that night. A team of my friends had come down to support me and they were all in on my gimmicks. I took everyone down to the beach front, around 8 or 9pm. I unveiled roses for every month which I had known Melissa, and I asked her to accept the key to my heart in the form of a pendant of a key attached to a chain link.

Her bashful demeanor was all I needed for reassurance. This was one of the happiest and most regretful days of my life. This night proved to me, the multiplicity of the human emotion. Though I was extremely happy that who seemed to be the love of my life at that time had basically accepted my hand in marriage, I was still in shock about the fact that my relationship with my second encounter with love had really and truly ended. It was as if our union solidified the fact that there was no turning back now. The love I had known for three years was finally over.

With love,

12/2/14

To the Universe,

At the time of this entry, my heart is suffering from its fifth encounter with love. As I write this, she sits in front of me, oblivious and rightly so. I know not the meaning of love, but it is safe to say I have mastered the emotion of infatuation, and at this point in time, I am deeply infatuated with this one.

This encounter is tricky to say the least. She is not used to my kind of love and she is younger. The mind is not as developed as mine, and it makes things a lot harder.

As I write, she is doing one of the things I admire about her the most. She is focused, she is resilient, she is both mature and immature, but right now she is being mature. I am a first year medical student and she is in my class. Since I was introduced to myself, I had always known myself to want to become a physician. Since I acquired the knowledge to understand what the world of a physician is like, I pictured myself ending up with a physician. Not to say that I am infatuated with her because she is pursuing the same career path as I am, but it plays a major role in the severity of my infatuation, as well as her attitude and natural ability towards her work and life in general. She is as quick as the speed of a bolt of lightning (130,000 miles per hour to be exact) and she is as intense as 30,000 amperes.

She appears to be mysterious and she thinks her tactics elude me.

She does not know that I play along with her games and I give her the satisfaction of thinking she has the upper hand. I am the worst kind of fool. I know better, but pretend I don't in an effort to somehow show her what she needs to know.

I know this isn't ideal and I know it most likely won't go anywhere. She never saw herself falling for a girl.

However, there are rare occasions where I feel like this may turn out to be more than what it seems. I get a taste of her soul whenever we interact, and when we have sex an eruption emerges from my core. The sex is explosive, our chemistry is unreal. I really sometimes wonder if this is truly real.

What haunts me now is the possibility of what we could be. I don't get the feeling that this is the here all end all. But I get the feeling that this encounter may be something worth experiencing.

With love,

18/12/14

To the Universe, with love.

That night, that night, THAT night. Was it THE night? Or was it one of the THE nights? That night, it was everything. It was unreal, it was surreal and it was so real. Moments like those are the ones people live to die for. The moments that make you feel like you're so alive that you're ready to die, that you're so happy that you could cry, and you're so lucky to be alive.

It was a perfect summer night. The air was filled with uncertainty and my heart was filled with adventure. Tonight, we were Cindy and Tim. Cindy and Tim are the perfect couple. The perfect couple created by my mind in order to circumvent the fact that the perfect couple which we would be, in reality will never be.

Even though there were many highlights of our impromptu rendezvous, one which rivals the best of them, was the exact moment we drove onto the beach. The look on her face could not be forged nor duplicated. It was as if she had just stepped out of real life and onto the pages of a fairytale. The wonder and amazement in her eye made me realize I was doing something right. I felt her appreciation and I felt her soul emerge from her body as her eyes beheld the magic of the view and ambiance of that particular beach at half past eight. Her soul came out to meet me that night and it was just as beautiful if not more than I had expected.

As I stared out into the ocean and poured her the first glass of wine, I knew I was exactly where I wanted to be and exactly where I should be. I watched her as she held the wine glass so delicately. As she stared into the distance, her soul was unfolded and revealed to me.

She kneeled behind me and put her hand across my chest and held me. I felt like I belonged to her.

I felt like I was her Tim, and she was my Cindy and for once, we were together and we were perfect and we were the only two people in the world.

One thing led to another and we were making love on the beach as the moon acceptingly shone down on us. It was one of the most complete and balanced moments of my life. I felt satisfied. I felt happy. I felt alive. I felt like I was finally living my life and doing the things that make life worth living. Life wasn't made to be ordinary. It was made to be extraordinary and I refuse to settle for anything less.

The Universe holds our dreams.

She was her, and I was me. And together we were for one night, Cindy and Tim.

7/4/15

To the Universe,

"I'm going to be happy and you're going to be happy and when we see each other we'll smile and only us will know why" - Cindy

The single most depressing statement I have ever heard in my life is above. It was so beautifully depressing that my soul wept, not the kind of depression that makes you sad and angry and violent and frustrated but the kind of depression that is beautiful. You feel so much love, that you're so gorgeously depressed at the thought that you won't ever be able to share the love you ought to with the person you should. The depression that comes with knowing that you'll never truly be happy. Sure, you will find happiness, probably the kind that's worth living for, but you won't have the happiness that's worth dying for.

 The thought of this statement makes me cry every single time.

I guess it's safe to say I found true love on my fifth encounter.

With love,

15/7/15

From MY Universe,

You meet people in life all the time.

But then;

There's that one specific person that your soul instantly clicks with.

You don't understand why, and you don't understand how.

You get this immensely overwhelming feeling, almost like a tachycardic feeling or maybe even bradycardic; both happening simultaneously.

Your heart feels as if it is going to burst through your chest.

My heart is weak and frail. This is why I need a break from the world. This relationship has by far been the hardest. Usually in midst of breaking up with my boyfriends, I imagine my new approach to life.

A life without them. A better life in fact.

I always seemed to have a plan until now.

This is indeed hard because in every aspect of my future I see you in it.

I see you as the person I call at random hours to gossip with, the person I feel the utmost comfortable with. The person who makes me smile, even when I really don't want to.

My lip quivers hiding from blushing because I don't want you to see the brightest smile ever invented because then you'll know just how much I love you.

This is not an ideal situation and it will never be and it must be avoided.

You Alex, are God's angel and you were created to do great things.

I know you'll be depressed and frustrated but just remember it will be worth it. I'm honored to even have known you as a person Alex.

You've taught me so very much and I listened to everything. You will be an amazing surgeon and a role model to many.

I wish our relationship would have stayed on a friendly level or even progressively went back to that point, but I will forever respect your wishes.

Tonight, I thought to myself, this movie would have been amazing with Alex or I wonder what Alex is doing. The guy I was with had to ask me if I was even watching the movie as he watched me constantly check my phone.

Anyway that's beside the point.

I do not want you to live in misery and Alex I am erased from your life.

Please, enjoy your life. I'll be gone for a while.

Depression for me is an understatement right now. I will be alone for at least a week, so if you think I've died and feel pity you don't need to. My charger is gone and I will not be getting another.

You probably hate me and I probably do deserve it.

I am truly sorry for making your life hell. I'm sorry for not being how you want.

You are truly my moon and my stars and my whole sun.

Goodbye Alexa.

With love,

Cindy

21/8/15

From MY Universe,

I'm up all night in bed. Confused. Depressed.

All I can think of is you spooning me every night; about how I want to cling on to that for as long as I can. Ridiculous right?

I'm going to tell you the truth about guys. Remember today when you said you try to see other girls but you can't? It's the same concept. I find a guy attractive and nice and respectful so I try. When I try I realize every single damn time that they don't seem to ever match up to you.

I do flirt to see if there is a spark. But the truth is I feel lost without you.

When we really got together for that brief moment, I didn't find it a challenge to not flirt with others. That's because my love for you is so great that it surpassed any attraction.

I appreciate everything you've given me. The love, the friendship, the everything.

You've said that we can finally be friends so I'm glad you can finally be my friend. But the sad truth is I can't just be your friend.

My family is the one thing that means more to me than our love right now. Our love is something they'll never accept. A great part of my happiness comes from the acceptance of my loved ones sadly.

Honestly I wish we could just run away as you said and build a hut and sell coconuts and have an easy life but the sad truth is life is just not easy. And it will never be.

I want you to be happy and we both know if you decided to do this, this is what's going to make you happy. So, in that case I wish you all the happiness in the world.

If I simply want to be happy right now I would choose you every single time but in the long run we won't be and the scars would become deeper and deeper.

I have the ability to use my mind to control my heart to some extent which is why I'm even able to recognize that this won't work otherwise there would be no issue.

Alex honestly I swear to God I love you with all my fucking heart and I would clean every orifice on your body with no hesitation; if you were disabled I would bathe you with no problem; if you needed to shit I would gladly wipe your ass.

I could never scorn you which expresses how comfortable I feel.

I just love everything and every single piece of you from your peas head to your dry feet.

And God knows I will always love you.

God fucking knows.

You are the rock I lean on. I'm sorry if hurt you, that was never my intention on this Earth. All I ever wanted was to give you everything you want, and I'm so sorry I failed to do that.

This is by far the hardest thing I'll ever have to do in life. This MBBS exam has nothing on what we have or had I suppose.

So I guess I can get through that as well.

I figure this email will probably annoy the shit out of you and I'm sorry if that's the case.

You always say millions of men see me. I hope you bear in mind that there's only one person I see.

The difference is that I look at them but you Alex, I SEE YOU. I really see you.

Every time I try to let go, I cannot.

But I will have to sooner than I thought. I fucking love your guts. Have a wonderful day when you wake up.

I hope this at least made you chuckle because that smile is worth everything.

Have a HAPPY day and don't let anything bring you down.

With love,

Cindy

22/08/15

To MY Universe,

No one person's words have the ability to make me cry like yours. As I write this I can barely see the words I'm typing as my phone is riddled with tears.

I'm so devastated right now that I really don't have much to say.

You're right.

This needs to be done.

I don't know how I'm going to live without you, but at this point I genuinely have to try.

This situation has emotionally destroyed me. I don't even want to feel anything for anyone else. At this point I really just want to be alone. I've been hurt a million times before and I've reacted in more extreme ways. But this by far is the greatest pain I have ever had to bear.

Everywhere I go and everything I do or see reminds me of you. Today I went to get a case for my phone and I just bought you one without thinking.

I don't how I am going to get over you, but I have to try.

You are my soul mate. Nothing has ever been as clear to me as that, and I'm truly sorry that we didn't get a chance to be Cindy and Tim.

There's one thing I can promise you, I will never stop loving you.

I hope you find what you're looking for. I really hope u do. You deserve all the happiness in the world and I'm just so sorry that I couldn't give it to you.

With love,

06/02/14

To the Universe,

Lately I haven't been ok. I have been coping. But I haven't been ok. I have had a history of letting everything build up to the point of combustion inside me. I refuse to speak to anyone. I refuse to find a human outlet.

This is my outlet.

I don't want to be an alcoholic like my father. However, it is really the only thing that gives me some relief from the speed of the thoughts inside my unconscious mind crashing upon my cranium.

I want a beer, but..

I woke this morning with a mission to be ok.

It's safe to say I got my life together this morning, no matter for how brief a moment it may be. I cleaned my room, took a long shower, properly groomed myself, washed the millions of armamentarium left in the kitchen that I have been putting off for weeks and I made a schedule for my day.

Enough of the boring stuff. How am I feeling? Sober. Sobriety.

I miss my family. But I have grown so numb towards family that I don't feel how I am supposed to feel. My Grandmother. My number one.

I hope she will understand how I truly feel, and I hope she can differentiate between my actions and reality. God bless her soul.

My mother and my father. I hope they know that I forgive them. I love them, no matter what. They taught me the meaning of the word unconditional. Your soul is connected to some people. You love them without condition. I have passed that test. There is definitely no condition which would make me stop loving them.

My youngest sister (that I know of). You are going through your most crucial years without me. I wish I could be there more to guide you. I wish I could comfort you, I wish I could encourage you, I wish I could help you with your homework. My soul is just not in a position to right now. My intentions are good and I hope you will understand.

Got a strange call last night. At about 2:46 am I received a call from who is now known to me only as my secret admirer. Will I ever meet her? Only time will tell.

Back to my emotions. I feel as though I am in limbo. I have most things I want, but most importantly I have everything I need at the bare minimum. I have my own space, I am pursuing the career of my dreams, I have food, I have shelter, I have money and I am helping people in my community. I should be satisfied right? I am grateful, extremely grateful to my Creator. I have come a very long way. But I am not happy, I am not satisfied. Why? Something's missing.

I'm not sure how to deal with this chronic feeling of emptiness. It is as if I need one more gear to have the car functioning properly. Right now it's at 65%. That one piece of equipment will bring it up to speed. Why are humans so insatiable?

How do you function properly until you can save enough money to buy that piece of equipment?

You don't.

You make do with what you have.

That's exactly what I will do.

I grow impatient most times, but I bear in mind that nothing happens before its time.

Until we meet again.

I want a beer.

15/8/14

Time, the greatest healer of ALL wounds?

They say time heals all wounds.

That may be so, but some wounds don't deserve to be healed.

My Granma passed away in April, and I can tell time from now to stay away from me.

I don't want to be healed.

I don't deserve to be healed.

She deserves to not only be remembered, she deserves to be felt.

She was such an inspiration, such a good person, that it would be an injustice if time took the liberty to heal my wounds. I want to cry, I want to scream, I want to shout, I want to feel. Every time I think of her, a tear must come to my eye, a tear because the world lost a person who was so great.

My mind must race with memories so prominent that I must stop and question where I am. I cannot afford for her existence on Earth to become just a memory. It has to be a legacy that continues living.

The death we know, is the disappearance of the flesh. And the flesh only.

If you've felt a love so strong, that you almost feel like you cannot get over, don't try to get over it. Don't settle for the cliche saying that time heals all wounds. Accept the fact that some wounds shouldn't be healed. Embrace the sadness, embrace the depression from time to time, because whoever you're missing might deserve it. Time should only focus on the wounds that need to be healed.

This one, it can leave alone.

With love,

7/7/15

To the Universe,

     And just like that I found the answer. And I found the answer in being alone. I've never understood how necessary it is to be alone. In fact, I think most of us don't.

We've always heard that being alone is hard but we need it. Why? In being alone, I lost all my distractions and was able to realize the real reason why I was unhappy. I've uncovered the sad truth about the fact that I have been brain washed by society to shape my perception of happiness into a form which does not actually suit me. I've always thought that I was just a relationship type of person, and that I always needed someone to keep me together and keep me sane. In being alone I realized why I felt that way, why I even needed to feel sane in the first place, why I would cling to bad situations and make irresponsible decisions to prevent loneliness. It is because I was unhappy and lost without even knowing, and for me, a relationship made me so happy that I didn't even realize I was lost.

We all have life goals. To study, to get a job, get a house, start a family. That's what has been instilled in our minds from before we were even born. But is that what we really want?

Growing up I convinced myself that I wanted to be a doctor, I wanted to help people, I wanted a beach house, a townhouse, a nice girlfriend, a black Subaru WRX and black sheets and then I would be happy. Sadly, these are all just things I think should make me happy but don't.

When you find yourself slowly achieving your goals one by one, but you're still grossly unsatisfied and desperately asking what's next, the you know you haven't achieved things that really speak to your soul.

If you're passionate about something you WILL know. When you feel REAL happiness, you will know. If you have to force something, from my experience, it's more than likely not worth it.

If you're just content, then sooner or later you will find yourself being unhappy. The human race is a remarkable species.

We weren't mean to be content.

We were meant to be happy.

With love,

22/03/16

To the Universe,

Today I'll write arguably the most important piece of writing I will ever write. Today, I write about my becoming.

It's funny how we plan everything with money in mind, as if money is actually the foundation of our lives.

Don't get me wrong, it is. Except it isn't.

I'm going to make my life plans without money in mind, because the concept of money is destroying us all.

When defining who you are and what you want, do it without money in mind. Then, your true desires will be revealed to you. Because after all, money is not as concrete as we think it is. It doesn't really exist.

The becoming is the beginning. The end is always the beginning. The end of the confusion, the questions, the wondering.

The becoming is the beginning of the rest of your life.

Your life stripped from the boundaries of societal walls.

The becoming is everything.

 I'm sure of it.

With love,

14/11/19

To the Universe,

Today I stumbled upon a letter I had written to you at the tender age of 14.

The more things seem to change, the more they stay the same.

"My name is Alexa-Rae Vanessa Clennon.

The people I love the most in this world are Omar Clennon, Arthur Clennon, Keesha Clennon, Ruth, Grace, Millicent, & Eric Miller, Nkechi Glanville, Sade Glanville, Lesley-Ann Robinson and Jhoneil Anderson.

Yes I love all those other people I'm supposed to love but not as much.

I am 14 years of age.

I have found that I am a very open minded person and I believe in free will.

I also have learnt through many, many deep conversations to respect people's decisions.

The world is made up of so many different minds who may look at things in a way you may have never even dreamed of.

I love football and most other sports.

I enjoy going out with family. No friends; like most people my age.

But I would not say that I am your typical teenage girl.

I hate girls.

I really do.

The only girls I can stand are the girls in my family and my close friends that are girls.

It is very unfortunate that I go to an all-girls school because of the kind of chaos that girls seem to cause everyday.

Trust me we girls are our own worst enemy.

For the most part of my life I have been a kid; a young mentally undeveloped child, seeking to be a child and simply just being a child.

Since I have become more mentally developed I have begun to miss the days of innocence and simplicity.

Being exposed to the harsh realities of life and being put in positions where you have to think not as a child but as someone who has responsibilities has lead me to lose my innocence.

One of my deep feelings of hatred lies in Christianity.

It is not the religion that I hate, tis the corruption in the religion. The hypocrisy. According to Christians; God gave humans the free will to choose whether they would like to follow God or not; so why does it have to be such a big deal if you're not a Christian?

Football has been a part of my life since age 6.

I'm pretty good.

Joke.

I'm alright; I grew up watching football.

Upon attending prep school I began to search for myself; unconsciously.

In my opinion that's the way life works.

I began playing football, refusing to wear dresses or skirts, hanging out with the boys. My two best friends were boys and we were inseparable.

I was searching; trying out different things and different personalities to find which one is ME.

Up to this day there is still an element of that personality which is stuck in the current personality I have now obtained. I love spontaneity. I hate knowing what I am going to do at 9:00am and then at 10:00am.

I love not knowing what's going to happen next.

That's what life is about; well partially life is about so many things.

It is really complicated and in my opinion, I doubt that anyone can truly grasp the meaning of life.

My biggest problem in my teenage life is not school or keeping up with the latest drama or backstabbing friends, but it is finding the true ME!

I really believe that I have a potentially superior mind but I am VERY LAZY!!

The main problem is finding that home that potential is locked up into and letting him out.

My main dilemma if u may is finding ME.

Only by doing that can I find out what I would really like to do in the future.

My brother has made sure that planning my future has become my main priority right now because time flies and I have only one year left in high school.

So as you can see time is flying quickly. I have to know what I want to do very soon but it is taking quite a while.

But that's life!!

One thing I truly like about myself is my ability to solve problems or rather how I look at situations.

I study people and how they react to problems.

My theory is that when you are faced with a tough situation, you best not mope or grieve.

Well they say grieving is healthy but not for too long.

You should just accept that this is how life goes. There is more heart ache and sorrow to go but you just have to find the best way out of each situation.

At 14 my major trouble is missing parties.

My brother however, made me look at it this way;

I'm only 14 so I have lots of years left to party.

So if I miss all the parties this summer I don't have to worry. I'm not going anywhere.

That's an example I guess.

But the point is to just chin up. Find the silver lining. There always is one.

The only problem I think I don't have the ability to deal with is death.

Only time can heal a broken heart so for now the only way to comfort a broken heart is by the passing of time.

Boy this started as a typing lesson; wow the product of insomnia.

Oh, music also inspires me.

Music is basically my WHOLE life.

I'm listening to music as I write this.

Maybe that's the reason behind this piece.

Wow.

Letting this out sure feels good.

People might say this is weird but guess what?

Alexa-Rae doesn't care.

I like that what people do or say doesn't really influence me.

I'm around a lot of girls 5 days a week that talk about sex and a large percentage of girls at my school aren't virgins and guess what?

That doesn't influence me a bit.

I'm smarter than that.

If the sexiest guy in the world told me to take a smoke and he'll go out with me guess what?

I wouldn't do it.

Nope, not me.

I love having MY OWN MIND.

If I drink I want it to be because I want to not, not because all my friends do it.

Don't get me wrong, I'm not perfect and I don't try to be.

I mean I cry and I hurt and I get hungry like everybody else.

But I look at things a bit differently.

Well, I'm gone now.

If I get this bored again I'll write some more.

This was fun, actually I will write some more.

Maybe I'll write a book someday.

LOOK OUT FOR MY NAME IN PRINT!!!

If u reached this far;

THANKS FOR READING!!

This might have not made any sense to you but this has given me some enlightenment and in some way fulfilment"

With love,

15/11/16

To the Universe,

I don't know if I was meant to write.

But who really knows anything?

However;

What I do know is that I can feel your toes curl as the love of your life caresses your ear.

I can feel the tears welling up in the back of your eyes as you think about how you're going to find your next meal.

I can think about how you feel as you watch your Grandma take her last breath.

I can breathe through your lungs as you feel the best kiss that has ever had the presence of gracing your lips.

I can hear the words that come to your mind but escape down the back of your throat and into your stomach as you watch the love of your life walk away for good.

I can feel everything.

My greatest curse is being human.

With love,

18/11/16

Cindy (2:02am)

When I'm dead come back and read these emails and look
at how ill-mannered and disgusting you were and in my
death I will not forgive you and it will probably be the only
place I can finally not care for you.

Tim (2:07am)

It will be the only place I will be free of you.
I hope one of us dies soon or falls in love.
It will the only place one of us can tolerate this horrible
existence.

ABOUT THE AUTHOR

Alex Clennon is a 24 year old poetry loving, psychology obsessed, philosophy enthusiast. Her main goal is to help people live their most authentic lives. Freedom is not just a concept, it is a choice. You can choose to live the life of your dreams. Let her help you.

 alexclennon

Alex Clennon

 alexclennon@gmail.com

 www.alexclennon.com

Printed in Great Britain
by Amazon